Dear Parents and Teachers,

In an easy-reader format, **My Readers** introduce classic stories to children who are learning to read. Nonfiction **My Readers** tell true stories and convey fascinating facts to children who are ready to read on their own.

My Readers are available in three levels:

1 **Level One** is for the emergent reader and features repetitive language and word clues in the illustrations.

2 **Level Two** is for more advanced readers who still need support saying and understanding some words. Stories are longer with word clues in the illustrations.

3 **Level Three** is for independent, fluent readers who enjoy working out occasional unfamiliar words. The stories are longer and divided into chapters.

Encourage children to select books based on interests, not reading levels. Read aloud with children, showing them how to use the illustrations for clues. With adult guidance and rereading, children will eventually read the desired book on their own.

Here are some ways you might want to use this book with children:

- Talk about the title and the cover illustrations. Encourage the child to use these to predict what the story is about.
- Discuss the interior illustrations and try to piece together a story based on the pictures. Does the child want to change or adjust his first prediction?
- After children reread a story, suggest they retell or act out a favorite part.

My Readers will not only help children become readers, they will serve as an introduction to some of the finest classic children's books available today.

—LAURA ROBB

Educator and Reading Consultant

For activities and reading tips, visit myreadersonline.com.

For Lenore, Frieda,
Izzy, and Rose

SQUARE
FISH

An Imprint of Macmillan Children's Publishing Group

Square Fish books may be purchased for business or promotional use. For information on bulk purchases,
please contact the Macmillan Corporate and Premium Sales Department at (800) 221-7945 x5442
or by e-mail at specialmarkets@macmillan.com

Library of Congress Cataloging-in-Publication Data Available

ISBN 978-1-250-03432-8 (hardcover)
1 3 5 7 9 10 8 6 4 2

ISBN 978-1-250-03436-6 (paperback)
1 3 5 7 9 10 8 6 4 2

Book design by Patrick Collins/Véronique Lefèvre Sweet/April Ward

Square Fish logo designed by Filomena Tuosto

Originally published by Henry Holt and Company, LLC, an imprint of Macmillan.
First MY READERS Edition: 2014

myreadersonline.com
mackids.com

This is a Level 2 book

Lexile AD460L

Lenore
Finds a Friend

A True Story from Bedlam Farm

Story and photographs by
Jon Katz

SQUARE
FISH

Macmillan Children's Publishing Group
New York

When Lenore came

to Bedlam Farm,

she was just a puppy.

None of the other animals

wanted to be her friend.

Even when Lenore got older,
the other animals
were not friendly.
The rooster
crowed at her.

The donkey tried to kick her.

The goats just jeered.

The dog named Rose
was too busy
to be Lenore's friend.

Rose had a job.

She took care of the sheep.

She kept them safe

while they ate grass on the hills

around the farm.

Once, Lenore tried
to lick Rose on the nose.
Rose didn't like it.
She had no time
for Lenore.

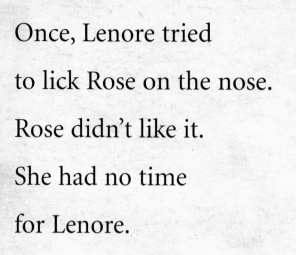

Lenore ran off

and hid in the grass.

Suddenly, she looked up.

A grumpy ram named Brutus

was standing right in front of her!

Lenore gave Brutus a big kiss on his nose.

Brutus had never been kissed before.

He turned away.

Lenore walked slowly
back to the farmhouse.
She felt sad.

The next day,

Lenore waited for Brutus.

She kissed him on the nose again!

At first, Brutus looked as if
he wanted to kick Lenore.
No one had ever tried
to be his friend before.

Lenore wagged her tail.
Brutus put his head down
near the ground.

Lenore kissed Brutus
on the nose again.

Then she rolled over
to show she wanted to play.

18

Soon, Rose came charging over.

She barked and nipped

at Brutus's legs

to make him go back

to the rest of the sheep,

where he belonged.

She growled at Lenore.

Lenore went slowly
back to the farmhouse.
She felt sad again.

But Lenore was not about
to give up on the first friend
she had ever made.

The next morning,

Lenore followed Rose and the sheep

to the pasture.

She wanted to find Brutus again.

Brutus was happy
to see his new friend.
He put his head down
so they could touch noses.

Soon, Lenore was happily eating grass

alongside Brutus—

and grass is not what dogs usually eat.

Rose came running up

to move the flock

and chase Lenore away.

But this time,

Lenore wouldn't move

and neither would Brutus.

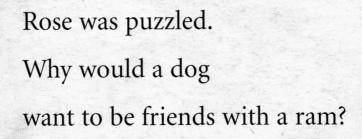

Rose was puzzled.

Why would a dog

want to be friends with a ram?

27

Rose watched them for a while,

then nodded once

and looked away.

She never bothered

Lenore and Brutus again.

Lenore finally had a friend.

This gave her a new idea.

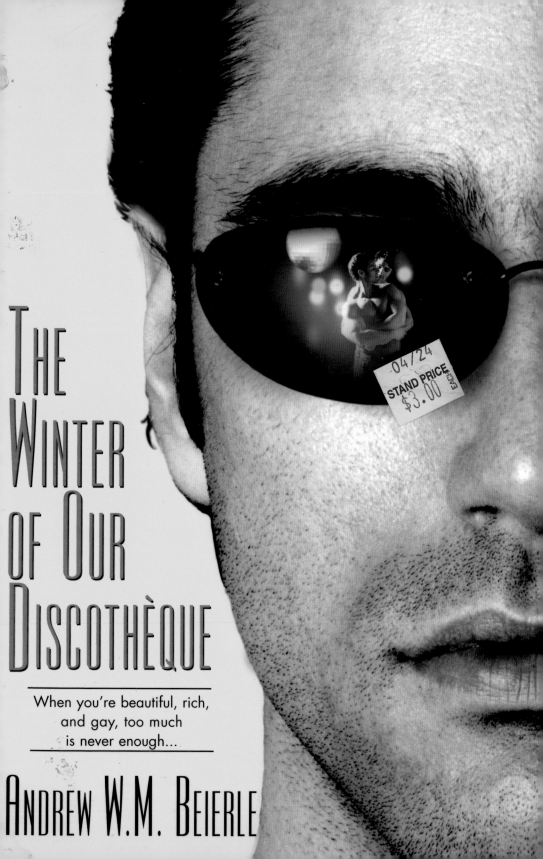

THE WINTER OF OUR DISCOTHÈQUE

When you're beautiful, rich, and gay, too much is never enough...

ANDREW W.M. BEIERLE